Woman: Created for Success

Titles in the School of the Word series:

A Life of Worship	John Johnson & Mike Stevens
According to Your Faith	Bryn Jones
Battle for the Mind	Stephen Matthew
Be Eager to Prophesy	Hugh Thompson
Called to be a Disciple	Dale Barnes
Christian Manhood	David Matthew
Effective Prayer	Bryn Jones
Essential Foundations	Hugh Thompson
Excelling as a Woman	Barbie Reynolds
Fulfilment in Marriage	Hugh & Rosemary Thompson
Go and Make Disciples	Hugh Thompson
Issues Facing Society	John Houghton
Living in the Anointing	Paul Scanlon
Money Matters	Stephen Matthew
More Than Conquerors	Don Silber
Realities of the New Creation	Dale Barnes
Secure in God	Tony & Margaret Howson
Successful Parents	Hugh & Rosemary Thompson
Woman: Created for Success	Barbie Reynolds
Woman: Living in Victory	Barbie Reynolds

Woman: Created for Success

Barbie Reynolds

Harvestime

Published in the United Kingdom by:
Harvestime Publishing Ltd, 69 Main Street
Markfield, Leicester LE6 0UT

First published by Harvestime
First printed July 1986
Reprinted January 1992

ISBN 0-947714-15-4

Typeset in the United Kingdom by:
ScribeTech Ltd, Bradford BD8 7BX

Printed and bound in the United Kingdom by:
BPCC Hazell Books, Aylesbury, Bucks, England
Member of BPCC Ltd

Increasing numbers of people are wanting to study the Word of God in depth. To go to a Bible college or seminary is not feasible for the majority, yet they desire more than the average church is able to provide in its teaching curriculum.

The book you are about to study is part of a library of components that together provide a comprehensive overview of the Scriptures in relation to life. Each book is complete in itself but is developed in such a way that the best result is experienced by studying it as part of the whole series.

We have produced the curriculum so that each component, in addition to its use as a personal study, can provide a seven-week teaching programme for study in church, home, college campus, school, military base, prison or any other group setting.

It is our prayer that you will be greatly enriched in your spiritual development through this book.

Bryn Jones
Founder — School of the Word

Getting the Most Out of This Study

This School of the Word study book is one of a series designed to relate Bible truths to everyday life. Each of the seven lessons starts with a direct search of the Scriptures and ends with a challenge to the student to apply the truths discovered. As the blank spaces left in Bible verses are filled in, the most important words and phrases stand out clearly on the page.

The material can be used in a number of different ways. It can form the basis of an individual study or be used in a group setting over a number of weeks. But experience has shown that it has the greatest benefit when a group of people study it together under a leader who is well prepared.

Tips for Leaders

If you are a leader planning to take a number of people through this study, you should consider the following:

1. Be prepared

It is essential that you do the whole study in advance yourself. This will help you to be conversant with the basic outline and have a feeling for the level of teaching based on it that your students can take.

2. Keep to the outline

It is important to keep to the outline contained in this study. This has been carefully designed to build principle on principle, 'precept upon precept' (Isaiah 28:10 RAV), with the eventual aim of the student becoming 'thoroughly equipped for every good work' (2 Timothy 3:17).

Whatever happens, don't allow your teaching to digress and become an opportunity to preach an hour's sermon!

3. Use your own experience

Even though you are staying with the outline, where possible introduce additional illustrations and applications drawn from your own experience. This makes the basic teaching more relevant to the local setting. In addition, you may wish to add more emphasis to certain points.

4. Avoid indigestion

Each lesson should take about an hour to complete. You may like to divide this into two half-hour sessions by arranging a short break for coffee and a chat halfway through. That way, the teaching is kept to manageable portions.

In some cases you may feel that the group discussion is of such vital importance to your local area that you want to spread each lesson over two weeks. If you do this, try to divide the questions at the end so that they are relevant to that week's teaching.

5. Have the right tools

Make sure that all the students have access to a copy of the New International Version of the Bible — upon which the book is based. Encourage them to fill in the blank spaces in advance but to leave answering the true/false questions until after each teaching session.

Tips for Students

Before you start the study you need to ask yourself: Am I really committed to growing as a disciple of Jesus Christ? If the answer is yes, then you're ready to proceed. Here are some immediate steps you can take to ensure maximum benefit from the course:

1. Determine your goal

This book is designed to help you achieve God's goal and destiny for you. It doesn't matter whether you are young or old, a recent convert or someone who has been a Christian for many years.

Today you are taking a step towards the fulfilment of your destiny.

Look ahead and see yourself as God desires you to be. Then confess your commitment: 'This is the kind of person I *will* become.'

2. Plan your progress

Your faith commitment to work through this book, and so take one more step towards becoming the person God intends you to be, must not only be pursued but measured in its progress. The apostle Paul said:

> *'By the grace given me I say to every one of you: Do not think of yourself more highly than you ought, but rather think of yourself with sober judgment, in accordance with the measure of faith God has given you.'*
>
> (Romans 12:3)

You know the kind of person you already are. You know the level of commitment you already have in your life. Now from this point determine how much time per day or week you are prepared to give to the study of the Word of God to achieve your goal.

At the end of each lesson in this study-book there is an opportunity for you to complete assignments and answer some Bible-based questions. This helps to fix the Word of God more firmly in your heart, and thus provide a reservoir of truth that the Holy Spirit can draw upon in the training of your life.

3. Recruit to the study course

Fellowship is one of the keys to Christian growth. The word 'fellowship' comes from the Greek word *koinonia*, which means to 'share things in common'.

Nothing will facilitate your progress as much as encouraging others to share in the same study programme with you, either on a personal basis or in a group. Share with each other the things you are learning and discovering in the Word of God and in life.

In this way you will be able to practise together much of what you study, and so strengthen each other in faith, just as 'iron sharpens iron' (Proverbs 27:17).

4. Set and maintain your standards

If this study is to be of maximum benefit to you, it must not be hurried. It is no use merely reading the written material and rushing the assignment. The book is designed to provoke you to your own searching and thinking, and to a demonstration of faith in God.

5. Check your progress

Once you have worked right through the book, ask your pastor or church leader to read through your answers. If he is satisfied that you have done your best to complete the questions, get him to send us a note to this effect. We will then forward a certificate for him to sign and present to you.

Your pastor is also the best person to monitor your progress and share your zeal to develop as a Christian disciple. If you are at college, university or in the armed forces, or for some other reason have no immediate access to a pastor, send us your book enclosing return postage and we will send it back to you with your certificate.

School of the Word
Harvestime Publishing Ltd
69 Main Street
Markfield
Leicester LE6 0UT
UK

IMPORTANT NOTE
This book should, ideally, be studied before the School of the Word title *Woman: Living in Victory.*

Contents

Unless otherwise stated, Scripture quotations are taken from the New International Version.

Other versions referred to in this series include the New American Standard Bible (NASB), the Revised Authorised Version (RAV) and the Amplified Bible (Amp).

Verses have blank spaces for you to insert the missing words as you follow the Scriptures. This will deepen the impact of the Bible in your life.

LESSON 1

God's Overall Plan

When God made woman, he created her beautiful and gave her, along with man, a position of honour and status beyond that of any other creature in his creation. She was made in *the image of God* – to express aspects of his nature that she alone could reflect.

Then sin came into the world. Fellowship with God was broken and woman lost much of her honour and status.

God is now in the business of restoring to his people the purpose, joy and freedom of being all that they were created to be. He's looking for women who not only understand his plan but are willing to co-operate with him in seeing it restored to them once again.

His plan incorporates every aspect of a woman's life: relationships, family, work, home, self-image, self-esteem, involvement in the church and personal growth and maturity.

Women need to be set free. Many are bound in chains to wrong beliefs and ideas. Others are prisoners to fear, failure and guilt. The truth of God's Word can set women *free!* Each one can become what she was created to be – a woman after God's own heart, who reflects his glory to the world.

1. A Magnificent Universe

'In the beginning _______ _______________ the __________ and the _________.'

(Genesis 1:1)

Even if we stretch our imaginations to the limits, it is impossible to picture accurately what the world was like when God first created it. But one thing is certain: he is a God who loves beauty and variety. Just look around you at all the beautiful things that he has made. He's never at a loss to produce something new and fresh and exquisitely wonderful.

2. The Final Masterpiece

When God finished making the seas and mountains, trees and streams, sun and stars, plants and animals, fish and birds, he saw that it was all *good* (Genesis 1:31). The luxurious smells and harmony of sounds put the finishing touches to the perfect environment for his final masterpiece.

'God said, "Let us make man in our image, in our likeness, and let them _______ over the fish of the sea and the birds of the air, over the livestock, over all the earth, and over all the creatures that move along the ground." So God created man in his own image, in the ___________ _____ _______ he created him; _______ _____ ___________ he created them.'

(Genesis 1:26-27)

God's final masterpiece, his great pride and joy, was to create an image or reflection of himself. It was one reflection with two component parts – male and female.

Men and women were created to be an expression of God himself. Together they were to demonstrate his heart and nature, rule and subdue the earth and fill it with people just like God.

They were to live in a perfect, unpolluted environment, surrounded by every blessing they could wish for. They were given authority over the works of God's hands and made an example to all the universe of God's goodness and love. They were the objects of God's greatest joy and pleasure, the recipients of his most extravagant love.

3. Man

In creating an image of himself, God first made one side of the reflection – man (Genesis 2:7).

He formed Adam out of the dust of the earth and gave him the job of discovery and exploration. He was to work the ground, make and identify things and join them together in an infinite number of combinations and varieties, and so bring further glory to God. Man's physical body thrives on work and he is fulfilled when he is working hard.

God prepared a specific garden or estate which, under God, Adam had the responsibility to care for (see Genesis 2:15). Adam's job was to be protector and keeper. He was responsible mentally, physically, emotionally and spiritually for everything in his care. It was this that gave him dignity and purpose in life.

When a man builds a house, plays with his children, works at his job or plants a field, he is doing what he was created to do. He is contributing to mastering the earth (Genesis 1:28). If, as he does these things, he reflects God's care and respect for creation and people, he will also enjoy the fulfilment God intended for him.

If, on the other hand, he distorts God's image, his work and reponsibilities in life will be a burden and frustration to him because he is not being a faithful mirror-image of God.

God gave Adam one specific command – not to eat a certain kind of fruit (Genesis 2:16-17). Although Eve was not yet created, God expected that in due course Adam would tell her about the command and enforce it. Women often feel they are solely responsible to God, but in God's original blueprint, *Adam* was held responsible for instructing *Eve*.

Adam had everything. He had total command of the world of nature and that of animals – plenty to occupy his time and an infinite variety of things to explore. But Adam was incomplete because he was alone. It was a bit like being in a giant animal sanctuary – it might have been fun for a while talking to the animals, but the only response he seemed to get was from the parrot – who merely repeated Adam's own words!

God isn't alone; Father, Son and Holy Spirit commune with each other. For a true reflection of God there must be a demonstration of unity, communion and companionship.

In order to demonstrate to Adam his incompleteness, God brought all the animals and birds to Adam for him to name (Genesis 2:18-19). Not one of them met the longing in Adam's heart for communion – friendship perhaps, but not communion.

4. Woman

Adam was asleep when God formed man's companion out of one of Adam's ribs (Genesis 2:21-22). When he awoke, there she was – flawlessly beautiful, perfectly moulded by God in his image and infused with God's own life. Adam could only exclaim:

> *'This is now bone of my bones and flesh of my flesh; she shall be called "woman", for she was ___________ _______ _____ _______.'*
>
> (Genesis 2:23)

She was part of him and together they formed a complete picture. She was:

☐ created from him and for him

☐ God's answer to Adam's need for a companion and helper

☐ someone to come alongside and share with him in the challenges of life

☐ one who felt as he felt

☐ a problem-solver with him

☐ one who shared his joy in discovery

☐ a love-gift from God

☐ the one who would bear their children, children who would follow in their parents' footsteps

a. No inferiority

Eve, which means 'life-spring', was in no way inferior to Adam. Any implications that she was second-best are unfounded in the light of God's Word.

Adam was her head. The fact that God the Father is the head of Christ (1 Corinthians 11:3) doesn't mean that Christ is in any way inferior to God. Rather, Jesus willingly submits to his heavenly Father. So it was with Eve.

The woman was created to be man's *helper*, not his *slave*. The Holy Spirit is given to God's people as a helper to come alongside them in their weakness (Romans 8:26). In a way, the woman is to be a helper to man.

Contrary to popular belief, Eve wasn't merely a spare rib! When Adam awoke from his deep sleep, he had an important part missing (Genesis 2:21). It was a part next to his heart.

Although men – and women – can live fulfilled lives as single people and shouldn't in any way feel inferior, they do have an element missing: a companion of the opposite sex. After his rib was removed to form Eve, Adam was *incomplete* without her.

With Adam and Eve there was neither superiority nor inferiority; together they made a perfect whole.

b. No problem with submission

Eve was totally free to be herself. In being what she was created to be, her whole being reflected God's heart and nature.

1. Helper

She was one who came alongside Adam, enabling him to fulfil his God-given commission.

2. Mother

God created her with a strong sex drive, which was a great joy to Adam. She thought he was the most fantastic thing in the garden. No doubt she told him so, too: 'You're so strong and handsome – so caring and protecting. And those muscles of yours . . . !'

The drive to mother her young was built right into Eve's physical body, and she had the emotional sensitivity to go with it.

3. Ruler and subduer

Eve gave full expression to all the creative drive God had given her. Alongside Adam, she brought that garden under their rule. They were excited together as they explored ways to harness the forces of nature. She loved working with him and for him.

5. Perfect Partner

It was God's ideal for man and woman to live in perfect partnership, each reflecting the qualities they were created to express (Genesis 2:24). As he watched Adam and Eve enjoying each other's company, in perfect harmony, God was satisfied. Like the rest of his creation, it was very good.

There were no secrets between Adam and Eve. With nothing to hide, communication came easily.

> *'The man and his wife were both ________, and they felt ____ ________.'*
>
> (Genesis 2:25)

They were *physically* naked and able to enjoy each other's body. They were *mentally* and *emotionally* naked and open with their thoughts and feelings. There was no pretence between them. They saw each other as they really were – and still weren't ashamed. They enjoyed the romance of each other's company.

There was no tension between them through trying to be anything other than what they were created to be. Self-rejection, self-centredness, guilt, fear, hurt and worry about being misunderstood were absent from the relationship.

They knew who they were and where they were going in life. They accepted each other totally. As a result, they had perfect peace and joy in one another because they were secure in a relationship that was to last for ever.

This was God's Dream Marriage – God's plan for perfect partnership.

* *

LESSON 1

God's Overall Plan

True or False

1. T F Adam was incomplete because he didn't have a companion.

2. T F God only created woman because he saw that man was lonely.

3. T F Eve was created primarily to meet Adam's needs and was therefore inferior to him.

4. T F In one sense, Eve had a similar role in her relationship to Adam as the Holy Spirit has to God's people.

5. T F Because Adam was created first and given responsibility in the garden, Eve's liberty was restricted.

6. T F Eve's strong sex drive was a hindrance to Adam.

7. T F Both Adam and Eve were called to rule.

8. T F God's plan for marriage was that there should be total harmony and openness between husband and wife.

Group Discussion

1. What were Adam and Eve commissioned to do together (Genesis 1:28)?
2. What was Adam's specific commission (Genesis 2:15)?
3. What was Eve's specific commission (Genesis 2:18)?
4. Could Adam or Eve, without God, be a true reflection of him (Genesis 1:27)?
5. In accepting that God's image is reflected equally in both men and women, what worldly attitudes towards each other will need to change?

Personal Assignment

1. Consider your own concept and understanding of marriage. Write down any differences between your concept and God's plan for marriage as described in this lesson.

2. Ask God to help you change your thinking and understanding on the role of men and women so that your expectations match his.

True or False

1.T 2.F 3.F 4.T 5.F 6.F 7.T 8.T

LESSON 2

What's Gone Wrong?

God put Adam and Eve in a place where they had complete and absolute freedom, the kind of freedom that mankind has searched for ever since. Their commission was to bring the earth under their control and to fill it with people just like themselves (Genesis 1:28). Obedience gave them the opportunity to show their appreciation of all that God had given them.

1. Satan's Part

The Bible teaches that Satan was once a glorious being who was second only to God in power and might in the heavenly realm. But he rebelled and decided to make himself like God. As a result he was thrown out of heaven (Isaiah 14:12-15).

Since then he has sought to establish his rule. Adam and Eve were the greatest threat Satan had had to face. They were given the earth to rule for God and their children would carry on that rule.

His scheming mind devised a three-pronged attack:

- ☐ at all costs get between Adam and Eve and their Maker
- ☐ divide their hearts from God
- ☐ inspire confidence in himself

Now read the results of his scheming in Genesis 3.

2. Eve's Part

Eve listened as Satan questioned the word God had spoken to her husband. God hadn't given her the command directly so she should have let Adam answer. Instead she misquoted and added to God's command, blunting its sharp edge:

> *'You must not eat fruit from the tree that is in the middle of the garden,* ***and you must not touch it****, or you will die.'*
>
> (Genesis 3:3)

Proverbs 30:5-6 warns against adding to God's word. The natural consequence of questioning, adding to, altering or denying God's word is deception and disobedience.

Eve then saw the fruit as Satan presented it to her. The tree was:

- ☐ 'good for food' (appealing to the appetite)
- ☐ 'pleasing to the eye' (a thing of beauty)
- ☐ 'desirable for gaining wisdom' (attractive to the intellect)

As a result, she was deceived into eating the fruit.

Eve suddenly felt that God was depriving her of the best thing in the garden. She mistrusted his goodness and doubted his love. She rejected God's way for her and did what *she thought would be best for her*.

Satan influences women in the same way today, deceiving them through their appetites, eyes and intellect into choosing a way that seems best for them.

3. Adam's Part

As head of his home, Adam received directly from God the command not to eat the fruit. He wasn't *deceived* by Satan's lies. Instead he disobeyed God's word *knowingly* and *wilfully*, choosing to yield to pressure from his wife. Man's first sin was listening to his wife instead of to God!

Satan works on men in the same way today, tempting them to abdicate or misuse the responsibilities God has given them.

4. The Consequence

The consequence of their sin is found in Genesis 3:7-19. Before, they were happy in God's presence. Now they knew instinctively that something was wrong. They were ashamed of their nakedness (v7). Instead of confessing openly their guilt and shame, they tried to hide it (v10). When questioned by God, they passed on the blame (v11-13).

In Genesis 3:14-19, God outlines specific consequences of their sin:

a. For Satan

Man and woman together were created to rule over Satan, but now they were to suffer under Satan as he sought to destroy them (v15). Jesus described his activity as similar to that of an armed robber:

> *'The thief comes only to _________ and _______ and __________ ; I have come that they may have life, and have it to the full.'*
>
> (John 10:10)

b. For woman

> *'I will greatly increase your pains in childbearing; with pain you will give birth to children. Your desire will be for your husband, and he will _______ _______ ______.'*
>
> (Genesis 3:16)

The joy and fulfilment God planned for woman in childbirth and motherhood would be overshadowed by conflict, pain and pressure.

The husband was now to rule over his wife. But the wife would no longer be satisfied with her God-given privilege of mirroring certain characteristics of God; she would desire her husband's role. This was the start of conflict between the sexes.

Sin came into the world by a woman. But by a woman *the Saviour* would come!

> *'I will put enmity between you and the woman, and between your offspring and hers; he will crush your head, and ______ ________ ____________ ________ ________.'*
>
> (Genesis 3:15)

The curse came by a woman. But by a woman would come the one who would *remove the curse*!

The liberty and freedom of the garden was lost by a woman. But by a woman one would be born to *regain freedom!*

By Eve's offspring, Jesus came to crush Satan's head. God never gave up on women!

c. For man

Genesis 3:17-19 explains that, because of disobedience, man's job of caring for his territory and eating the fruit of his labours would now be accomplished only by the sweat of his brow. It was the same job, but now accompanied by conflict and pain.

5. The Outcome

God was heartbroken. He had no option but to drive the man and woman from the special garden he had prepared for them as a place of fellowship and unity with himself. If we choose to live our own way rather than God's, we cut ourselves off from fellowship with God.

> *'Your iniquities have ________________ you from your God; your sins have ____________ ______ ________ from you, so that he will not hear.'*
>
> (Isaiah 59:2)

God is holy, and nothing unholy can stay in his presence. So the sword was stationed at the entrance to guard the way to the presence of God, the tree of life (Genesis 3:24).

6. Women Repressed Through History

History reflects Satan's hatred of women.

a. Before Christ

Hundreds of years before Christ, three major world religions were started that repress women: Confucianism, Buddhism and Hinduism.

b. Ancient Greece

In ancient Greece women were regarded as inferior to men and treated largely as chattels, while the purpose of a wife was merely sexual satisfaction and the production of children.

c. Judaism

God chose the Jewish people to be a nation through whom he would demonstrate to the world what he is like. In the early days women were honoured. Miriam and Deborah, for example, were involved in the social, political and spiritual life of the nation.

But later, the rabbis gave their own interpretation to God's laws and added new ones of their own. Attitudes to women became more and more repressive until, by the time of Jesus:

- ☐ a man was taught to give thanks daily that he was not born a woman
- ☐ women were not permitted to give testimony in court because they were considered unreliable witnesses
- ☐ women were not allowed in the inner courts of the temple
- ☐ women were forbidden to be taught the law lest they corrupt it
- ☐ women were not permitted to speak or sing in the synagogues

☐ talking with a woman was considered degrading for a man

☐ having a baby girl was considered to be a disaster

d. Present day

Even today, in many parts of the world, women are regarded merely as sexual objects or baby-producing machines, with no rights or dignity of their own. Satan's goal has been to destroy feelings of self-worth in women and spoil any reflection of God.

But God's plan is to restore women to their proper place of dignity and respect, as we will see in the next lesson.

****

LESSON 2

What's Gone Wrong?

True or False

1. T F Questioning or altering God's word leads to deception.
2. T F Eve felt that God was depriving her of what was best for her.
3. T F Adam was deceived into sinning by his wife.
4. T F The trauma and pain of childbirth are part of God's original plan for a mother.

5. T F As a result of the curse, woman became dissatisfied with her role of mirroring God's image and instead wanted to rule over her husband.

6. T F God promised that the woman's offspring would crush Satan's head.

7. T F God laid the blame for sin at Adam's feet because of his direct disobedience to God's command.

8. T F By choosing to live our own way, we cut ourselves off from fellowship with God.

9. T F The biblical teaching of submission of a wife to her husband is the cause of women being repressed.

10. T F The fact that women are considered inferior to men in most parts of the world is God's judgment on them.

Group Discussion

1. In what ways do women today feel deprived as Eve did?

2. Identify the areas in your own lives that are a burden and a 'curse' to you and consider how they relate back to the curse on Eve in Genesis 3.

Personal Assignment

1. Write down two things in your life that hinder you from reflecting God's nature. Pray and expect God to show you his solution as you study lesson 3.

2. Consider areas of your life where you are easily deceived. Ask God to help you deal with deception.

True or False

1.T 2.T 3.F 4.F 5.T 6.T 7.T 8.T 9.F 10.F

LESSON 3

God's Plan of Recovery

Before Adam and Eve sinned, they were perfect human beings. They lived in harmony with God and each other in a pollution-free environment. There was no disease, corruption or death.

When Adam chose to obey Satan, he and Eve received Satan's corrupt nature and brought themselves under his rule. From then on every person had the same nature and inherited spiritual death.

> *'Sin entered the world through one man, and death through sin, and in this way death came to all men, because all sinned.'*
>
> (Romans 5:12)

1. A Hint of Recovery

Before Adam and Eve left the garden, God demonstrated his grace (unearned favour) by providing them with a covering for their shame. They had been surrounded by life, but now death came: an animal needed to die in order for them to be covered by the skin. *God* clothed them – they themselves did nothing (Genesis 3:21).

In Jesus' story of the prodigal son (Luke 15:11-32), when the son came home poverty-stricken, the father ordered the servants to clothe him with the best robe. In a similar way, God clothes us with the best.

'He has clothed me with garments of salvation and arrayed me in a robe of ____________________.'

(Isaiah 61:10)

God himself gave the first gospel illustration right back in the garden of Eden! By clothing Adam and Eve, he was showing that one day he would save people from the awful consequences of choosing to obey Satan rather than God.

2. A Perfect Solution

God loved people so much and was so eager to restore fellowship with man and woman that he eventually sent his own Son, Jesus, who had a sinless nature, to be born as a human being.

Jesus was the fulfilment of God's promise to Eve that some day one would be born who would be bruised by Satan, but who would then crush Satan's head.

'The God of peace will soon __________ __________ under your feet.'

(Romans 16:20)

Jesus, like Adam and Eve, grew up in harmony with God and had free will. Like them, he was confronted by Satan's questioning of the Word of God (see Luke 4:1-13). But instead of yielding to Satan, he remained perfect and at one with God.

His purpose in coming to earth was to destroy the works of Satan and to bring eternal life. He died on the cross to free us from sin and its power.

> *'The wages of sin is death, but the gift of God is ____________ ________ in Christ Jesus our Lord.'*
>
> (Romans 6:23)

Satan's nature of sin and death in us can now be replaced by God's nature of eternal life. We can be free from all those consequences of sin that hold us back in life – things like fear, tension, worry, guilt, pride, self-consciousness, sickness, hurt, resentment, bitterness, jealousy and anger. We can be healed of our sicknesses and can know that the sting of death has been removed through Jesus (1 Corinthians 15:54-57).

3. Free to Start Again

> *'Just as through the disobedience of the one man the many were made sinners, so also through the obedience of the one man the many will be made ____________.'*
>
> (Romans 5:19)

The way back to God is open again! God's recovery plan not only makes it possible to return to God's original blueprint, but God actually designed it so that men and women gain far more through Christ than Adam lost!

4. The Dignity of Women Restored

In lesson 2 we saw how Satan's hatred of women has resulted in their worldwide repression down through history. Even God's chosen people, the Jews, had so added to his laws that God's attitude to women had been completely distorted.

a. Jesus sets the example

Jesus cut across the teachings of the rabbis, deliberately going out of his way to demonstrate the honour and status God bestows on a woman. Three women – all called Mary – illustrate this:

1. Mary, the mother of Jesus

Mary was given the incomparable privilege of giving birth to the Son of God (Luke 1:26-38). Imagine the ecstasy – and sobering sense of responsibility – that this young girl must have experienced as she was pregnant with God's precious Son!

2. Mary of Bethany

Mary of Bethany was the one who took an alabaster jar of expensive perfume – probably an heirloom handed down to her – broke it open and anointed Jesus in preparation for his burial. Jesus said that her act would be remembered wherever the gospel was preached (Matthew 26:6-13; John 12:1-8). What a tribute to her!

3. Mary Magdalene

Mary Magdalene had the great honour of being the first person to see the resurrected Lord Jesus Christ. Not only that, but he sent her to tell the other disciples about his resurrection (John 20:10-18).

b. Jesus' radical attitude to women

Unlike other teachers of his day, Jesus *taught* women and shared deep spiritual truths with them (John 4:21-24). He used women as illustrations in his parables (Luke 15:8-10) and referred to women who featured in the Old Testament, such as the Queen of Sheba (Luke 11:31).

He *healed* women even when, by doing so, he made himself unclean according to the law. This was the case with the woman subject to bleeding (Luke 8:43-48). When she touched the edge of his cloak, he didn't rebuke her, but encouraged and healed her, with love and respect. Immediately after that he raised a little girl to life (v49-56).

Often Jesus *served* others by doing what was considered to be women's work. He prepared a meal for the disciples, building the fire and gutting the smelly fish (John 21:9-13). He made the disciples serve a meal and clear it up (Luke 9:16-17)! He washed the disciples' feet (John 13:3-5).

He had a similar attitude to children and their mothers. He refused to be treated like a rabbi in having nothing to do with children. Rather, he rebuked the disciples for sending the children away and actively *encouraged* the mothers to bring their children to him (Luke 18:15-17).

Jesus also *cared* for women. He raised a young man from the dead because he had compassion on the widowed mother (Luke 7:11-15). In talking about the impending destruction of Jerusalem (a wartime crisis), he had in mind the pregnant and nursing mothers when he said, 'Pray that your flight will not take place in winter' (Matthew 24:19-20).

While he was carrying his cross, he expressed deep concern for the weeping 'unknown' and 'unimportant' women with him (Luke 23:27-29).

In contrast to the teaching of the rabbis of his day, Jesus taught that both father *and* mother were to be honoured. As if to emphasise the point, he repeats father *and mother* four times in just three verses (Mark 7:10-12).

Jesus never used the word 'subordinate' or 'subject' in connection with women. He treated them as his disciples. For example, he commended Mary for 'sitting at his feet' (Luke 10:38-42), a discipleship term used also of Paul, who sat 'at the feet of Gamaliel' (Acts 22:3 RAV).

c. In the early church

Paul was the first to teach men to love and honour their wives. Look at how important he considers that love to be.

> *'Husbands, love your wives, just as ___________ ___________ _______ ___________ and gave himself up for her.'*
>
> (Ephesians 5:25)

After Paul preached to a group of women in Philippi, one of them, Lydia, became a Christian and was baptised, with her whole household. She then helped establish a thriving church in her home. People were added and the church continued to meet under her roof (Acts 16:12-15, 40).

Many other incidents and examples in the New Testament demonstrate that the heart desire of Jesus is to restore women to the place of honour and dignity that God designed for them.

5. Free to Do His Will

Have you accepted the gift of freedom from doing things your way? Have you returned to God and become his beloved daughter? If not, why not start life today?

First, acknowledge that you can't please God by *anything* you do. The Bible says that even our best efforts are like filthy rags to God (Isaiah 64:6). Only Jesus' personal death on the cross for your sin and sickness could pay the price that God's justice requires.

Then ask God to forgive you for living in rebellion to his way and tell him that you want Jesus to rule your life from now on. Consciously hand over every area of your life to him. Give him everything – relationships, attitudes and motivations.

Receive his forgiveness and his washing of you deep down inside. Let him put a new heart in you (see Ezekiel 36:25-27), a heart that is pliable and willing instead of one that is hard and unyielding.

Thank Jesus for dying for you and for making you his child. Find out what the Bible teaches about water baptism and the baptism in the Holy Spirit.

6. The Process of Recovery

With every man, woman and child who returns to him, God starts a process of recovery. He begins to clean up the mess that sin has made. Step by step he restores that person until he or she becomes as clear as a mirror, reflecting God's very life and image.

When that happens, people start working in real harmony together instead of grimly putting up with each other. Parents learn about raising their children to love and serve God. Children, for their part, become secure in their parents' love. Broken relationships are healed. It's a life of discovery and excitement!

Marriage partners need to begin the process of overcoming the barriers that sin has raised. These barriers are not only physical, but mental, emotional and spiritual as well. God's recovery programme involves a process of 'becoming one'.

Adam and Eve were 'one' in the garden. Adam called Eve 'woman' because she was taken out of him (Genesis 2:23). He was her source, but from then on woman would be *man's* source through childbirth. They belonged together.

> *'A man will leave his father and mother and be united to his wife, and they will ____________ ______ flesh.'*
>
> (Genesis 2:24)

In the remaining lessons we'll be considering how women can co-operate with God in his restoring to them the ability to rule and reign – alongside their husbands, if they are married, and in harmony with men in the church and in the world, whether they are married or single.

Jesus prayed that our unity as Christians might be a demonstration of the fact that he is God's answer for the world. Let's ensure that it begins with unity between man and woman.

> *'I pray also for those who will believe in me through their message, that all of them ______ ____ ______, Father, just as you are in me and I am in you. May they also be in us so that ______ __________ ______ ____________ that you have sent me.'*
>
> (John 17:20-21)

LESSON 3

God's Plan of Recovery

True or False

1. T F If Adam and Eve hadn't sinned, they would never have come under Satan's rule.

2. T F Satan tried to get Jesus to doubt the truth of God's Word, but Jesus remained perfect.

3. T F Jesus died in order to give us eternal life in heaven and it's only there that we will be free from fear, sickness and sin.

4. T F God has a recovery plan that makes us better off than Adam and Eve.

5. T F Jesus accepted and put into practice the social and religious norms of his day regarding women.

6. T F God wants his people to be a reflection of himself on earth that will demonstrate to the world what he is like.

7. T F Jesus prayed that we would be one with him so that we will be fit for heaven.

Group Discussion

1. In Christ we have gained more blessings than Adam and Eve lost. Look up the following scriptures and discover

together some of the 'added extras' we have received: Ephesians 2:4-7; 4:22-24, 25; 1 Peter 1:4; Romans 5:20-21; 8:17; 1 Corinthians 6:2-3; Hebrews 2:10-12.

2. Jesus was radical in his attitude towards women, cutting across the prejudices and social norms of his society. In what ways can women today demonstrate to those around them the radical nature of God's attitude towards them?

Personal Assignment

1. Read section 5 again. Have you returned to God yet? If not, identify why you haven't. You may want to seek the help of a Christian you know. If you *have* returned to God, begin to thank him for the different aspects of his great salvation.

2. In what two ways do you most need to change in order for God's reflection to be seen in you?

3. Having specified the main areas of your life that need to be changed, actively open yourself to God to change you in those areas.

True or False

1.T 2.T 3.F 4.T 5.F 6.T 7.F

LESSON 4

Man's Commission: To Rule

In understanding our role as women, it's important first to discover what God expects of men. In the next two lessons we'll be looking at various aspects of the man's role and how it affects women.

1. Created to Rule

God gave Adam authority over the garden before Eve was even created (see Genesis 1:26). Her rule subsequently supported his. Adam was accountable to God for everything that went on there.

> *'The Lord God took the man and put him in the Garden of Eden to ________ it and ________ ________ of it.'*
>
> (Genesis 2:15)

God still requires men to give account for the areas of responsibility that he has entrusted to them. He intended every man to have a place where he alone is boss and where his authority is not continually threatened, a place where his care and work give him a sense of personal satisfaction.

In a way, a man is a reflection of God when, like his Creator, he experiences a sense of achievement in seeing that what he accomplishes is 'very good' (Genesis 1:31).

2. Rule in the Home

God holds a man accountable for everything that happens in his home and intends that he should know the dignity and self-esteem that come from exercising the rule and authority of God there. Consider what this might include:

i. The choice of town, neighbourhood and house in which he (and his family) lives.

ii. The decor and upkeep of the house and, where there is one, the care of the garden.

iii. The local church to which he belongs.

iv. The choice of a marriage partner, the number of children they have and the decisions concerning their children's upbringing and welfare.

v. In the case of a married man, how the money is to be spent and when; the choice of family holidays and leisure activities; his family's health, protection and security; and his wife's spiritual growth and development (Ephesians 5:25-28).

God instructed Abraham to bring direction to his children and his household, teaching them to walk in God's ways.

> *'I have chosen him, so that he will ____________ ______ ______________ and his ______________ after him to keep the way of the Lord by doing what is __________ ______ ________, so that the Lord will bring about for Abraham what he has promised him.'*
>
> (Genesis 18:19)

God will bless and prosper any man who leads his family in the ways of God and who takes full responsibility for all that happens in his home. Consider some of the difficulties a man often faces when he tries to do God's will in this matter:

a. Feminist influence

The feminist movement has sought to do away with the concept of the man as the breadwinner and the decision-making head of the household. Society at large is in confusion and won't necessarily support him in his lead. Relatives, neighbours and friends may misunderstand his actions.

b. Reversal of roles

Women are often brought up to believe that home and children are their responsibility. When the children are young, women frequently assume total responsibility for handling them and this is continued as the children grow up. Many women resent any 'interference' from their husbands.

c. Resistance

There is no satisfaction for a man in being head of his home when his wife, and perhaps his children, resist him either in word or attitude. If his decisions are constantly being questioned, he may feel that leading his home just isn't worth the trouble.

A wife who undermines her husband's confidence by reversing his decisions, or by making it clear that she feels she's more capable of leading in the home than he is, makes it hard for a man to do what God expects of him.

d. Demand for perfection

A woman who requires a man always to get it right before she shows love and respect makes a man feel like giving up before he even starts. Some wives become ill, deliberately mishandle the children, lose their temper or go on a spending spree if their husbands make a decision that is not along the lines of what they want.

A common failing in a wife is to pressurise her husband into doing things that she feels should be done at a time when she wants them done. Her husband often gives in under such pressure. Then, when things don't work out the way she expected, she blames him!

Abram experienced this when his wife, Sarai, who was unable to conceive, put pressure on him to have a child through her Egyptian maidservant, Hagar. Later Sarai blamed Abram for the hateful, conceited attitude Hagar had towards her (Genesis 16:1-5).

Instead of having such an attitude, you can cultivate a *positive* approach:

i. Understand and accept from your heart that God has commissioned men to rule – to take overall responsibility – even though in some men the desire to do so has been so crushed that little evidence of it remains.

ii. Understand that some men are lazy or afraid of failure and don't want to take their God-given responsibilities. It will require time, prayer and loving support on the part of God's people, including women, for them to see that their greatest satisfaction and fulfilment lies in accepting their role. Learn to love them as they are and let God change them.

iii. Understand that a woman who constantly threatens or undermines a man's authority may cause him to become stubborn, argumentative, domineering or selfish in order to maintain that authority. When he feels support and encouragement and his position isn't threatened, he's much more likely to use his position to serve others.

iv. Understand that, because God intended every man to have a particular place for which he is accountable, men seek such a place for that desire to be met.

If you're married, make sure that your home is available to meet your husband's needs in this area. If he has a lot of authority in his job, he may be more willing to delegate much of the responsibility at home. If he has little or no authority at work, exercising authority at home may be of greater importance to him.

v. Ask God to give you his desire to see every man you know exercising his God-given authority and responsibility.

Remember that a woman who pressurises a man to take on more responsibility than his faith can handle is likely to be a hindrance to him and may even be the cause of nervous trouble or illness. A woman who criticises or, through her own fear, causes a man to stop short of his full potential will likewise cause him to be unfulfilled and fail in his reflection of God.

vi. A woman placed in a position of authority over a man doesn't reflect God's original intention.

Like Adam in the garden, men are frequently tempted to 'pass the buck' and let a woman lead them. By prayerfully cultivating an attitude of respect for the position God has given man, a woman can go a long way in encouraging men to take their place of rule under God.

Instances in Scripture (such as Judges 4:4, 9), in the church and in society where women have successfully fulfilled a leadership role – even where God has anointed that leadership – still don't reflect God's original intention.

3. Rule at Work

God intends that, even in a world where unemployment is at an all-time high, men should thrive on hard work.

> *'The sluggard craves and gets nothing, but the desires of the diligent are ______________ ______________.'*
>
> (Proverbs 13:4)

> *'When we were with you, we gave you this rule: "If a man will ________ __________, he shall ________ ______."'*
>
> (2 Thessalonians 3:10)

A woman who encourages a man in his job, whether it is paid employment, voluntary help or work for Christians in the church, is helping him to do what is pleasing to God. God intended that man should know the satisfaction of doing a job well and, in the case of the married man, shouldering the responsibility of providing for his family.

Women who try to prove that they can do better than men are

a hindrance to man's knowing the satisfaction God intended for them. Some women *are* better at their jobs than their male counterparts but their *attitude* of superiority and competitiveness is undermining to men and thus a hindrance to God's purpose.

Some men see their job as a 'calling'; for others it's simply a means of providing for their needs. Some jobs are rewarding in themselves, while others have no inbuilt satisfaction.

Women need to understand what a man's job means to him so that they can be a support and encouragement to him in it:

a. Male relations

If you have a father, brother or working son, never give him the impression that his job is unimportant. Also, help him to know that you feel he is God's means of blessing to you. A sense of purposelessness results from feeling unneeded.

b. Fiancé

If you're engaged to be married, learn to appreciate what God has called your fiancé to be in terms of his job and the rest of his life. Avoid the three components of the traditional wedding, 'Aisle, altar, hymn' (in other words, 'I'll alter him')! Don't try to make him something he isn't called to be.

c. Husband

Wives who complain about their husbands' jobs for whatever reason – too long hours, too little pay, no prospects, too risky

– deprive them of the satisfaction and self-esteem of work designed for them by God.

If you're married and you don't know what your husband does all day, find out and take an active interest. Appreciate the long hours he puts in. Learn to be content with the money he brings home.

Appreciate the trouble he goes through just to get to work – traffic, trains, bus queues, people, parking, or rising early to milk the cows, plough the field or make deliveries on time.

Understand the pressures he faces at work. Perhaps there is competition just to keep the job at all. The level of emotional stress is high in today's competitive society. Make sure you're not adding to his pressures by comparing him with other men.

Make his home a place of encouragement where he finds appreciation and acceptance and is free to be all that God intended him to be.

d. The unemployed

In a world where unemployment is once more escalating and where paid employment is increasingly difficult to find, it's still important to remember that God commissioned men to *work*. Work doesn't have to be paid employment in order to be constructive and productive.

Men who are unemployed are susceptible to feelings of guilt and loss of self-esteem, even though their lack of a job may be through no fault of their own. Women who even secretly despise an unemployed man are a hindrance rather than a help to his becoming the person God intends him to be.

Even when paid employment isn't available, any man can be provoked and encouraged to do a good six days' work serving those in need in the church or community.

4. Rule Through Care and Protection

> *'The Lord God took the man and put him in the Garden of Eden to work it and ________ ________ of it.'*
>
> (Genesis 2:15)

God designed man with an inbuilt desire to protect and care for women. When a man responds to God's will for him in this, he gains a feeling of manliness and self-respect.

In past generations men weren't considered men unless they were willing to die to protect their wives and families. But this desire has been virtually destroyed in many men because of women's determination to live independently and refusal to accept protection from men.

Gone are the days when the gallant man would put his cloak over a puddle to protect a woman's feet. Now it's rare for a man to give up his seat on the bus or train to protect a woman's tired legs!

In order for men to fulfil again their commission to protect and care for women, especially those for whom God has given them responsibility, women will need to humble themselves and acknowledge that they *need* the care and protection that God has provided for them.

Women need to recognise that an air of independence and scorn of men is destructive of the very things God intends men to be.

a. Physical protection

If men were exercising their God-given commission to protect their women, it's unlikely that there would be so many reports of rapes, muggings and assaults.

Women who insist on lifting and carrying heavy loads or who do heavy manual work are not receiving the protection for the physical health of their bodies that God intended. God created men with the potential for greater physical strength than women. Manliness and self-respect result when a man uses this strength to care for and protect women.

b. Emotional protection

Some women are prone to depression and continually find themselves in a battle against moodiness. A woman who allows her husband or brother to help her out of self-centred depression is wise. Disregarding the advice of her husband or brother, or secretly despising it, destroys his desire to protect her and she will be the loser.

Women generally are susceptible to emotional 'ups and downs'. Men see things more objectively. Let them speak into the things you're worried about. If you're single, make use of the pastoral care God has provided for you in the church. Both married and single women can benefit from their Christian brothers' more logical and clear assessment of situations.

Man's objectivity is a God-given balance to woman's emotional sensitivity – a gift for women to take advantage of.

c. Mental protection

Women, by nature, want to help others. Constant requests to help at school, church and various clubs and societies can cause undue pressure. Women who take on too many things become frustrated and their physical and mental health may suffer.

Learn not to be so independent that you lose the protection God has provided in the men who are close to you. Hear God's 'No' through your husband or leaders. The result will be happier, more relaxed women and an increased desire in men to protect those whom God has commissioned them to care for.

d. Spiritual protection

Women also need protection spiritually. The Bible clearly teaches that wives should ask their husbands any questions they have (1 Corinthians 14:35). For single women, home groups or small informal meetings of the church provide opportunity to share their concerns or ask for prayer on spiritual matters.

A man will be motivated to take spiritual responsibility for those in his care when help is sought from him. Children will follow their mother's example in going to the man of the house for spiritual guidance and help.

God made you, as a woman, with a different role from man. You're not inferior. Without you, man is an incomplete expression of the heart of God. Learn to embrace the role that God has given you.

LESSON 4

Man's Commission: To Rule

True or False

1. T F Men are required to give account for the areas of responsibility that God has entrusted to them.

2. T F Every man, Christian or non-Christian, will experience a sense of fulfilment when he accepts his God-given responsibility to be head of his home.

3. T F Wives must give account for how their homes are run and their children behave.

4. T F A wife's duty is to assume overall responsibility for the home if her husband seems unwilling to take the lead.

5. T F A man should find satisfaction in doing a job well and, if married, in providing for his family.

6. T F Wives who don't understand men's drive to rule through care and protection can destroy the very things that God intends men to be.

7. T F All women are independent spiritually and should never need to go to a man for spiritual guidance and help.

Group Discussion

1. Consider together the men with whom a woman comes most into contact, for example, father, husband, boss, brothers and those in the church. Share some ways in which your attitude and behaviour needs to change as a result of what you have studied in this lesson.

2. How can a woman help a man who isn't fulfilling his God-given responsibilities? What kind of attitude will be the most helpful to him?

3. Pray for one another, especially for those who have special prayer requests relating to this lesson.

Personal Assignment

1. Part of a married man's commission is to make provision for his family's needs. List ways in which a woman can help her husband or father enjoy providing for her and the family.

2. If you are married, consider your husband's job. Does it require physical, mental or emotional energy? List things you can appreciate and compliment him on regarding his work.

3. If you are single and support yourself:
   a. Thank God that you have a special place in his heart (Isaiah 54:5) – in a special way he wants you to know him as your husband;
   b. Consider the men with whom you most come into contact, such as at work or in the church. What attitudes

do you personally need to guard against that could be a hindrance to men finding real self-esteem as men? Settle with God what you are going to do about it.

4. Write down any areas of responsibility that you have been carrying but which you now see God intends your husband, boss or church leaders to carry. Ask God to help you make the necessary adjustments in a sensitive and loving way.

True or False

1.T 2.T 3.F 4.F 5.T 6.T 7.F

Man's Commission: To Increase and Subdue

In lesson 4 we saw that God commissioned man to rule in his home, in his job and in his care and protection, particularly of dependants. In addition, God told Adam and Eve:

> *'Be fruitful and increase in number; ________ ______ ________ and __________ ____.'*
>
> (Genesis 1:28)

1. Fill the Earth

Without the sex drive, men and women wouldn't be able to fulfil their joint commission to 'fill the earth'.

God built this drive right into our physical bodies, yet Satan has sought to spoil sex, distorting people's view of it. The pervading attitude for generations was that sex was sordid, unpleasant and even sinful.

Today, by contrast, it is flaunted on almost every advertisement board and paraded daily on our TV screens. But God wants to restore to his people a healthy understanding and appreciation of their sexuality.

a. Sexuality and single people

It's part of God's plan that people should, in marriage, enjoy a permanent sexual relationship with someone of the opposite sex. But single men and women, too, have strong God-given sexual desires. How can they best handle them?

1. Understand the opposite sex

Accept the fact that God has made men different from you, not only in their physical appearance, but also in the way they react sexually.

Women tend to be stimulated by a romantic atmosphere, by feeling loved and cared for, by the security of a strong, loving man.

Men, on the other hand, are *visually* stimulated. Just the sight of a woman can trigger off the physical effects of sexual arousal. Temptation for them comes through the presence of a woman, through their own vivid imagination and through looking at films, newspapers or magazines with provocative or suggestive contents.

Because of this God-given sexual response, men need to learn to control sexual arousal by avoiding visual stimuli and by learning to 'take captive every thought to make it obedient to Christ' (2 Corinthians 10:5). But single (and married) women can go a long way towards helping their brothers in Christ to avoid temptation.

> *'Let us stop ______________ ______________ ____ ________ ______________. Instead, make up your mind not to put any ______________-__________ or ______________ in your brother's way.'*
>
> (Romans 14:13)

Think before you wear clothing that might lead to unnecessary temptations for men. Clothes that could cause particular problems include tight jeans, revealing tops and short shorts, immodest swimsuits, skirts with deep slits, blouses with plunging necklines and other clothing deliberately designed to reveal the woman's body.

Remember, too, that men have strong imaginations. It's for this reason that striptease is so much more popular among non-Christian men than looking at nude bathers. Avoid clothing that tantalises, even if it doesn't reveal too much.

Here is an opportunity to serve your brothers in Christ – not just to follow a legalistic dress code.

2. Learn both to accept and to control sexual feelings

Men usually have no difficulty understanding sexual temptation. They face it on a regular – if not a daily – basis. Single women, on the other hand, may easily deny or repress their God-given sexual feelings. Instead, face up to them honestly, control and discipline your imagination and be careful in choosing the things you read and watch.

3. Develop healthy friendships

Many men today have formed wrong concepts of women. Some think of them as mere objects of sex. Others fear them because of bad experiences in the past or simply don't understand them because they've never had a sister.

Here is another opportunity for single women to help their brothers in Christ. Get to know men in your church – preferably in group situations – without the pressure of pairing off or 'going out' with someone.

For your part, learn to see the opposite sex as people or friends, not just 'men'. This is especially important if you have a wrong concept of men because you were sexually abused as a child or are being sexually harrassed at work. God wants to heal the hurts and help you learn to relate to men once again.

b. God's plan for sex in marriage

God made woman to be physically attractive to man and put in her the desire to be loved by man. In marriage, man and woman can give physical expression to their God-given desires.

Lovemaking was God's idea. It brings fulfilment and is to be enjoyed. Husbands are told:

> *'May your fountain [the body parts that produce life] be blessed, and may you rejoice in the ________ ____ ________ ________. A loving doe, a graceful deer – may her breasts satisfy you always, may you ever be ________________ ____ ______ ________.'*
>
> (Proverbs 5:18-19)

Only in marriage can a man and a woman find true sexual fulfilment free from the fear, shame, jealousy and hurt that come by its use outside of marriage.

> *'Marriage should be honoured by all, and the marriage bed kept pure, for God will judge the adulterer and all the sexually immoral.'*
>
> (Hebrews 13:4)

Sex is a dimension designed by God to enhance the oneness of a husband and wife. He intends them to be totally dependent on each other for sexual satisfaction. A well-adjusted sexual relationship reduces tension and friction in other areas of marriage. The love bond created between husband and wife brings a sense of security and well-being to children.

How, then, can you as a wife contribute to a happy sex life in marriage?

1. Meet your husband's needs

Your husband has God-given sexual desires that need to be met. If you refuse, he may be tempted to turn to forms of self-gratification such as masturbation or sexual perversion.

Sex in marriage should involve *giving* rather than *getting*. If you seek to meet your husband's needs, and he seeks to meet yours, you will have a happy, enjoyable sex life.

A wife tends to withhold sexually when she doesn't feel valued and loved by her husband during the rest of the day. A husband tends to withhold when his feelings are hurt or he doesn't feel esteemed by his wife. But the provision of sexual satisfaction is a *duty:*

> *'The husband should fulfil his marital duty to his wife, and likewise the wife to her husband. The wife's body does not belong to her alone but also to ______ ______________. In the same way, the husband's body does not belong to him alone but also to ______ ________.'*
>
> (1 Corinthians 7:3-4)

It is interesting to note that the words 'alone' and 'also' are not in the original Greek, making Paul's statements even more pointed.

2. Avoid feeble excuses

'I'm too tired.' 'I've got a headache.' 'I don't feel like it.' These are some of the excuses wives (and husbands!) use to avoid meeting their partner's sexual needs. Deal ruthlessly with selfishness, which is often at the heart of such excuses. God designed the sexual relationship so that the more you put into it, the more you receive back.

3. Get things right

You may have lost interest in sex because you have argued with your husband and not put things right. Without regard for his own faults in the situation, ask your husband to forgive you for the wrongs you have committed against *him* during the day.

> *'Do not let the sun go down while you are still angry, and do not give the devil a foothold.'*
>
> (Ephesians 4:26-27)

Agreeing to disagree leads to strain, tension, frustration and ultimate breakdown in the relationship.

4. Face up to fear

Fear can hinder your sex life, particularly fear of not being able to meet the needs of your partner. If you are afraid of frigidity, face up to your problem. Talk it over with your husband. If, on the other hand, your husband is afraid of premature ejaculation or being impotent, help him to discuss it. Seek to encourage him, help him to relax and remember never ever to make fun of his sexual performance.

5. Be real

Don't try constantly to achieve an imaginary standard of what *ought* to happen in lovemaking. Instead, enjoy your husband and seek to bring pleasure and fulfilment to him in the best way you can.

That doesn't mean that you must settle for second best. Be honest and open with your husband. Tell him your feelings and needs in this area. Learn from his comments and work at continual improvement. Explore fresh ways of fulfilling each other.

6. Don't be ignorant

If you've never read a book on sexual technique in marriage, get one and read it together. (A good one is *A Touch of Love*, by John and Janet Houghton – Kingsway Publications.) Get to know the differences in sexual responses between you and your husband.

Your husband may not know about your rhythmic emotional cycles. If, during part of your cycle, you're not easily aroused sexually, he may misinterpret this as rejection of him. Help him to understand the way God made you in this area.

7. Nothing but the best

Always remember that God made man with a strong sexual drive and desire. If you despise your husband's sexual desire you wrong him, making him feel guilty or inadequate. If you fulfil it, he is more likely to be a success in other areas of his life.

Know too that God wants *you* to be sexually fulfilled. Even if you have what seems to be a major problem, determine to settle for nothing but the *best*. It gives God pleasure to enable you to be fulfilled.

2. Subdue the Earth

Little boys often love to pull things apart to find out how they work. Their desire to know 'what makes it tick' is part of a wider desire to bring things under their control.

God commissioned both Adam and Eve to subdue the earth. In lesson 6 we'll consider how a woman can fulfil her commission to subdue the earth. But how does God expect a man today to fulfil this part of his commission?

i. In a man's work, God expects him to do the best job he can do, rather than just 'get by'.

ii. If there are challenges to face at work, a man will be fulfilled in meeting them. For example, he may devise some new method in order to overcome a difficult task.

iii. A man is fulfilling his God-given commission when he doesn't give up in the face of pressure and difficulties, but sticks at a job in order to accomplish what he knows has to be done.

iv. A man is doing God's will when he realises that a part of his home or family is in disorder and he determines to bring order into it.

v. When a man sets aside time to work on something he is responsible for, such as house repairs or tidying the garden, he is fulfilling his commission to bring under his control things that would otherwise become a mess.

The forces of nature, if left unattended, would destroy mankind. But God put the drive in men and women to bring these forces under their control.

Sin has made some men and women lazy and irresponsible. Others have used their God-given drives for wrong and selfish ends. But God can restore the desire to put things right and once again live God's way.

Men's response to challenge differs. In some, it produces a response of: 'If anyone can do it, I can.' In others, the response is slow or negative: 'I don't know if I can manage it,' or: 'I'll try sometime.'

The difference may be determined by *past experience*. A man may have a negative reaction to challenges because of a mother who demanded perfection or a wife who is hypercritical.

A man who used to like challenges may have given up because *others*, such as his wife, *lack confidence in his ability. Fear of failure or financial insecurity* may also stop him from accepting God-given opportunities to fulfil his commission to subdue the earth.

A woman who understands that God wants a man to take responsibility, and to bring things under control, can go a long way towards helping him to achieve this end.

Never ridicule or denounce an idea that a man (even a young man such as your son) may have when confronted with a challenge. Encourage him to try. If it doesn't work, he'll gain from the experience. Encourage him to try again.

Many women live miserable lives because they covet their husband's position as head of the home. Even Christian women, because they know what the Word of God says, can technically obey and submit to their husband's authority but secretly despise his leadership and thus question God's appointed order.

In the church, women can have the same undermining attitude to their leaders, but in the end it is the women who are the losers.

> *'Obey [your leaders] so that their work will be a joy, not a burden, for that would be of____ ____________ ____ ______.'*
>
> (Hebrews 13:17)

If a man isn't fulfilling his God-given commission to subdue the earth, he will feel unworthy. This can lead to such problems as: nervous disorders or psychosomatic illness; a lack of drive; fear of throwing himself into a job because people will find out how incapable he is; withdrawal; cruelty; dependence on alcohol or drugs; lack of confidence in applying for a demanding job; and unwillingness to accept the leadership role he has as a man.

If, on the other hand, you help the men you know to accept their commission from God to subdue, they will grow and mature in God.

Wives, when your husband asks you to do something, be thankful. Compliment him when he takes the lead.

When you see a man in need of encouragement to do what God expects of him, give him the praise he needs. Be a sister to your brothers in Christ, married or single. Pray that the men you know will find the joy of being real men, reflecting God's image.

LESSON 5

Man's Commission – To Increase and Subdue

True or False

1. T F A truly spiritual man will not be concerned about sex.
2. T F The sight of a partially naked woman can easily stimulate men sexually.
3. T F Single women need to deny and suppress their sexual feelings.
4. T F Single people are destined to a life of frustration because sexual fulfilment is not open to them.
5. T F God has made only one outlet for the enjoyment of sex that eliminates fear, shame, jealousy and hurt.
6. T F If a married couple are giving themselves to Christian work, it doesn't matter if they don't have time for lovemaking.
7. T F The more a wife puts into her sexual relationship with her husband, the more she'll get out of it.
8. T F God commissioned man, along with woman, to subdue the earth and put in him the drive to control the forces of nature.

9. T F God intended every man to know the joy of discovery and mastery of his circumstances.

Group Discussion

1. In what ways has the so called 'sexual revolution' threatened to spoil God's plan for sex?

2. Consider the effects on a man who works with women who are constantly trying to show how much more capable they are of doing his job than he is. What should such women do?

Personal Assignment

1. Acknowledge before God if you have had any sexual relationships or experiences that you now know were displeasing to him and you have never put right. Confess them to God, ask his forgiveness and receive his cleansing. Consider whether you need to ask forgiveness from the other person.

2. If you're single, ask God to show you if you are being a stumbling-block to Christian men either by the way you dress or by your attitude towards them.

3. If you're married, consider what you most need to improve on in your sexual relationship with your husband. Remember that God always has more to show you in this area, however long you've been married.

4. Are you making it difficult for the men you know to bring order and change into their lives? What are you going to do about it?

True or False

1.F 2.T 3.F 4.F 5.T 6.F 7.T 8.T 9.T

God's Design for Woman: A Helper

In these last days God is raising up, not just individuals or even individual families, but a large company of men and women who will again work as one, ruling and filling the earth with people like themselves. Women have an important part to play in this.

1. What is Woman's Commission?

Woman was commissioned by God to be a helper and mother and, with man, to rule and subdue the earth. In this lesson we'll consider the first of these.

'I will make a ____________ suitable for him.'

(Genesis 2:18)

The word 'suitable' means 'corresponding to'. God designed a helper corresponding to a man physically, emotionally, mentally and spiritually. She was one who wholeheartedly co-operated with him in working out God's plan.

God has planned it so that, in marriage, the husband and wife need each other in order to fulfil their own God-given roles. Similarly in the church, men and women work together in harmony so that each fulfils his or her God-given task.

2. What Kind of Helper?

There are a number of Hebrew words that are translated in

English as 'helper'. The Hebrew word used in Genesis 2:18 means 'ally'. It is never used to mean a servant. In fact, on a number of occasions, it is used to describe God:

- ☐ Exodus 18:4: God is a helper in the sense of being a *deliverer*.
- ☐ Deuteronomy 33:7: The word is used to mean a *refuge* or *defender*.
- ☐ Psalm 33:20: Here it means a *protector*.
- ☐ Psalm 89:19: It is used here to mean a *strength*.

There was nothing second-rate or feeble about the helper God brought to Adam!

If you're married, are you close enough to your husband to know his thoughts and feelings and thus be his deliverer, refuge, defender, protector and strength?

Two wives in the New Testament illustrate a right and a wrong way of being an assistant or source of strength to their husbands: Sapphira and Priscilla.

a. Sapphira – a bad assistant

In Acts 5:1-11 we read about Ananias and Sapphira, a married couple who had agreed together to deceive the church about the amount they had received for their land. They wanted to be seen to be doing the right thing, but their hearts weren't right with God.

When challenged, Sapphira went along with her husband's deceit, covering up for him instead of speaking the truth. The result was that she joined her husband in being struck dead by God!

In matters of morality and righteousness, God expects every woman, married or single, to stand accountable before him. As she does so in meekness and humility, she may be the very means God uses to convict a man of his sin.

> *'Be submissive to your husbands so that, if any of them do not believe the word, they may be won over without words by the ____________ of their wives, when they see the __________ and ____________ of your lives.'*
>
> (1 Peter 3:1-2)

b. Priscilla – a good assistant

Aquila and Priscilla were tentmakers, a husband-and-wife team who first gave hospitality to the apostle Paul in their home in Corinth (Acts 18:2-3). Later, they travelled together with Paul teaching and instructing the Christians (Acts 18:18, 26).

When writing a letter to the Romans, Paul sends Priscilla and Aquila his special greetings, calling them "my fellow-workers in Christ Jesus' who had 'risked their lives for me. Not only I but all the churches of the Gentiles are grateful to them' (Romans 16:3-4). Priscilla was a wife who had aligned herself with her husband and, as a result, God had been able to use them as a team.

How about you? Are you a helper and a support to the men with whom you come into contact: your husband, father, pastor and brothers in Christ? Are they encouraged just by your presence? Do you help them to fulfil their God-given commission?

> *'Her husband has ________ ____________________ in her and lacks nothing of value. She brings him good, not harm, all the days of her life.'*
>
> (Proverbs 31:11-12)

Eve enjoyed total freedom and fulfilment in her role as Adam's helper. She was indispensable to him. Together they worked as a team and mirrored the image of God on the earth.

3. What About Submission?

When Eve chose to obey Satan rather than God, she betrayed her role as helper and became a subject.

> *'Your desire will be for your husband, and he will rule over you.'*
>
> (Genesis 3:16)

The word used for 'desire' here is the same as in Genesis 4:7, where it describes sin's desire to rule over Cain. It suggests that, as result of the curse, Eve wanted to rule over her husband. But, says the Lord to Eve, '*He* will rule over *you*.'

When Jesus died to free us from sin and the power of the curse, he opened the door for woman to be restored once again to the honour and dignity of reflecting God's nature in being a helper. She is no longer one who needs to be 'ruled over' but, like Eve before the Fall, she is a *voluntary* helper.

Have you come to terms with the way God has arranged the family and the church? Do you know where you fit? Ask God to make you a willing, voluntary helper.

4. Headship

When a person becomes a Christian and comes under the rule of Jesus, he or she must learn to accept the people that God has placed in positions of authority. They include church leaders, parents, husband, teachers and police.

It's especially important to ensure that you place your life under the spiritual oversight of those *God* has chosen for you (see Hebrews 13:17). They aren't there merely to exercise their power, but to lead, protect, provide and care for the people who submit to them.

Two people can't drive a car at the same time. If they have the same destination in mind, one will be a co-traveller and will give all the support necessary to help the one in the 'position' of driver to do his job. The driver doesn't see his position as one of 'power' but as providing a means for both to reach their destination safely.

This is how God intended the authority relationship between men and women to work, husbands to wives, leaders to the church and employers to employees. For example:

> *'The husband is the ________ of the ________ as Christ is the ________ of the ______________, his body, of which he is the Saviour.'*
>
> (Ephesians 5:23)

Headship is not an excuse for lording it over people but a means of *serving* them. God intends headship to provide the *service of leadership*.

Submission to God's appointed order is submission to God. He planned headship and submission in order to create the optimum environment in which we can flourish – in every way. For example, a wife's submission to her husband is really submission to Christ.

> '*Wives, submit to your husbands as to the Lord.*'
>
> (Ephesians 5:22)

The woman who is truly subject to Christ knows the immense joy and freedom of being subject also to those he has given to lead, provide, care for and protect her.

A wife can genuinely and willingly give first place to her husband as an expression of her love and devotion to God.

A woman in the church can accept and respect her church leaders, knowing that they – not her – are accountable to God for the decisions they make.

Woman is free once again to be what she was created to be – a helper whose heart throbs with love and desire to serve the one who gave his life to set her free. Submission is a natural heart response to the rule of Jesus: 'I want to please him with *all* my heart.'

5. Respect

Men and women are commanded by God to show respect for others (1 Peter 2:17), including employers, teachers and others in authority, whether they deserve it or not. Wives are also instructed to respect their husbands.

> *'Each one of you also must love his wife as he loves himself, and the wife must ________________ ________ _________________.'*
>
> (Ephesians 5:33)

The Amplified Bible uses the following synonyms to describe the word 'respect' in this verse:

1. 'Notices him'

When her husband comes home from work, she is there to greet him. He feels appreciated and wanted in his home. She's never too busy to give him time and attention when he needs it. She's not taken up with her own affairs at his expense.

2. 'Regards him'

She makes it her business to find out how he likes the home kept, the meals prepared and the children to behave. She makes sure that she is moving in unity with him as she carries on her daily life.

3. 'Honours him'

Honour means 'to give weight to'. She doesn't take lightly his wishes and opinions but considers him, and all he is involved in, to be of great importance.

4. 'Prefers him'

When it comes to choices, she is willing to lay down her desires and give him preference. She makes sure he knows she prefers him to anyone else!

5. 'Venerates and esteems him'

This is an attitude of heart that she cultivates, learning to esteem him because he is her husband. The way she speaks of him to others will convey her esteem.

6. 'Defers to him'

She doesn't act on her own initiative for selfish ends. She is an initiator on behalf of her husband. She is his delegated authority in the home and upholds his decisions.

7. 'Praises him'

She looks for things which she can *genuinely* praise. She guards against flattery, which is insincere praise given from a selfish motive. She rejoices to see him become a man fulfilling his God-given commission and shows her appreciation by telling him.

8. 'Loves and admires him exceedingly'

This is something the Holy Spirit desires to work into the heart of every wife. God wants her to be 'head over heels' in love with her husband and for that love to be growing all the time.

Although the above is addressed to wives, the Bible commands *everybody*:

> *'Be devoted to one another in brotherly [and sisterly!] love. Honour one another above yourselves.'*
>
> (Romans 12:10)

Be a true helper and know the dignity and honour of being a reflection of the very nature of God. In doing so you will be a delight to his heart and bring glory to his name.

LESSON 6

God's Design for Woman: A Helper

True or False

1. T F Men and women are commissioned by God separately and can therefore fulfil their tasks independently.
2. T F God's plan is that men and women should co-operate *wholeheartedly* in working out his purpose.
3. T F People who think being a 'helper' is second-rate or degrading to a woman don't understand the meaning of the word.
4. T F When Jesus sets a woman free from the curse, she no longer needs to submit to anyone.
5. T F God's design is that headship and submission would produce the optimum environment for us in which to flourish.
6. T F A woman who submits is no longer free to be what she was created to be.
7. T F Women who are married should respect their husbands, even if they don't deserve respect.

Group Discussion

1. Consider together the fact that submission has nothing to do with inferiority or superiority. It is the heartfelt

acceptance that God's best for our lives lies in being what women were created to be. It is the total absence of any desire to exercise authority over men or usurp the role God has given them.

2. In what ways can a woman be: i. a protector and ii. a strength in the church?

3. How was Jesus a comfort and strength to his disciples? How can we as women be a comfort and strength in the same way?

Personal Assignment

1. Set aside time to consider before God whether you have ever really accepted, from him, your role as a 'helper'.

2. Ask God to show you two ways in which you can be obedient to the command in Romans 12:10 this week. Wives, consider carefully whether you are 'respecting' your husband in the Bible's definition of the word given in this chapter. Are there any changes you need to make in your relationship with your husband?

True or False

1.F 2.T 3.T 4.F 5.T 6.F 7.T

LESSON 7

God's Design for Woman: A Mother and Co-Ruler

1. Being a Mother

'Adam named his wife Eve, because she would become the ____________ ____ ______ ______ ____________.'

(Genesis 3:20)

Eve means 'life-spring'. Adam and Eve together were commissioned to 'be fruitful and increase in number; fill the earth and subdue it' (Genesis 1:28). The union of male and female has always been God's method of producing life. The woman's role from the beginning was to bear children. Man was to be the provider.

The drive to 'mother' is one of a woman's strongest instincts. Even if a woman doesn't have children of her own, the drive is often expressed in mothering someone else's children – or even in mothering a pet or taking care of plants.

God designed woman with a desire to 'mother' in order that his purposes in the earth would be fulfilled. Recognising and accepting this fact helps a woman come to a healthy understanding of herself and how God made her.

If you're married, guard against the desire to 'mother' your husband. A man who is 'mothered' inappropriately will become dependent and fail to exercise his authority and rule as the man God intended him to be.

There is, however, an appropriate mothering role for older women in relation to younger men and women. Paul writes:

> *'Greet Rufus, chosen in the Lord, and his mother, who has been __ ____________ ____ ____, too.'*
>
> (Romans 16:13)

Many younger people today, both men and women, have been deprived of real love and care in childhood. There are many opportunities for women, who themselves have become secure in the love of God, to care for them, bringing them through to security and self-acceptance.

2. Life as a Single Woman

In spite of the fact that there is a trend in modern western society to give more prestige to the single life than to marriage, there is still a certain stigma attached to the truly single woman. The stereotype is someone who is desperately lonely, always miserable and constantly searching for a man.

But in God's kingdom this needn't be the case. A Christian woman – married or single – can only find true contentment and fulfilment in accepting God's plan for her life today. His will for the single woman may change in the future, but the important thing for her is to accept and fulfil his purpose in her life *now*.

Marriage may never be part of God's plan for some women.

If this is the case, their greatest blessing and fruitfulness for God will lie in the fact that they have been *selected* by him to remain single.

> *'An unmarried woman or virgin is concerned about ______ __________ ____________: Her aim is to be devoted to the Lord in both _____________ and __________. But a married woman is concerned about the affairs of this world – how she can ___________ ______ ______________.'*
>
> (1 Corinthians 7:34)

In a very special sense, the single woman knows *God* as her head. She has a unique relationship with him which is for ever. She is set apart for him – devoted to him and to the interests of his kingdom.

There is plenty of scope to 'mother and nurture' in God's house where spiritual babies are being born all the time. These new Christians need hours of love, care and attention to bring them through as mature men and women of God. Single women have an invaluable part to play in this.

If you're single, why not make yourself available to your church leaders in this area?

3. Subduing

Men and women were jointly commissioned to subdue the earth (Genesis 1:28). We saw in lesson 5 that this drive is expressed by bringing the forces of nature under our control and making them work for our good.

A woman fulfils her commission in this area by accepting the challenges that daily life brings her. She sees each new challenge as an opportunity to gain experience and competence in the tasks God has given her to do.

Whether it is cooking a meal, writing a letter or using the office computer for the first time, she seeks to excel at the task in hand. She learns to be creative and lets faith rise in her heart as she faces the demands of each new day.

Read Proverbs 31:10-31. This husband had found his wife trustworthy. She had shown herself worthy of his full confidence in handling all the affairs he had entrusted to her. Every woman – married or single – should seek to become trustworthy to the men she knows.

The husband in Proverbs 31 isn't in any way threatened by his wife's competence. This is because she 'brings him good, not harm, all the days of her life' (Proverbs 31:12). Are you a threat to the men at your work, home or church?

Consider some of her other attributes which show how she is fulfilling her commission to 'subdue the earth': she's a hard but joyful worker (v13); she makes her own clothes (v19); she plans nutritious meals for her family (v15); and she rises early to make the packed lunches and get everyone off to school and work in peace (v15)!

In her business dealings she has godly ambitions to increase her profits (v18); she's a hard and diligent worker, industrious with her time (v17); and she's a buyer of real estate – letting God make her prudent with money and always looking for ways to be creative with what she has (v16).

Her husband develops to his full potential (v11); she doesn't fear old age (v25); she's praised by her family and community alike (v28, 31); she's a woman who fears the Lord and is to be praised (v30).

Is your home (your room, your apartment) displaying the order of God?

How about work? For many women, their work will be carried out in and from their homes. But for others it involves paid employment.

If you're single, your job is a means of being involved in and serving the community at large. It's also a training ground for producing godly character, another opportunity for you to reflect the image of God to a needy world. Do you see it as such – or simply as a means of earning money?

If you're a married woman in paid employment, you may need to ask yourself whether or not it is a help or hindrance to the well-being of your family as a whole.

No doubt, the extra money is important to you. But there are other important factors to consider. For instance, does your husband *want* you to have that job or did you pressurise him into giving his permission reluctantly? Would you be prepared to give up work if he wanted you to?

Are you working as a 'helper', serving him in your joint call, or hindering him from providing for his immediate family in the way God expects him to (1 Timothy 5:8)?

Whether you're in paid employment or not, are you managing your time or does your time manage you? Whether it be a lazy attitude to overcome, or stepping out in a new business venture, are you facing each challenge and subduing every obstacle in your life with *eagerness* and *faith*?

> *'Whatever you do, work at it with ______ ________ __________, as working for the Lord, not for men, since you know that you will receive an inheritance from the Lord as a reward. It is the ___________ __________ you are serving.'*
>
> (Colossians 3:23-24)

4. Ruling

God blessed Adam and Eve and commissioned them together to rule the earth. Adam was given the primary charge to rule the garden and Eve's rule subsequently supported his. God's will is done when man and women rule together.

We saw in lesson 6 that God has appointed men as head of their families (I Corinthians 11:3), and that headship provides the service of leadership.

A woman who accepts that God has chosen particular men to provide, care for and protect her (whether in her family or in the church) will know the peace and security that God intends. But women also have a part in ruling. Jesus said:

> *'These signs will accompany those who believe [including women]. In my name they will __________ ______ _____________ . . . they will place their hands on _________ _____________, and they will get well.'*
>
> (Mark 16:17-18)

Women, as well as men, have been commissioned by Jesus to rule over 'principalities and powers' in the spiritual realm (Ephesians 6:10-13). Behind some sicknesses, fears and disruptive circumstances there are evil spiritual forces. The Holy Spirit can show you their root so that you can take authority over them in the name of Jesus and bring the rule and order of God into your daily life.

a. In the home

The single woman in her home is subject to Christ as her head. She is free to rule her own home, carrying out her tasks as efficiently and creatively as possible, putting Jesus and the building of his kingdom first. She can either waste her time or use it to be fruitful and effective (Matthew 25:14-30).

In getting married, a woman chooses voluntarily to place herself under the authority of her husband.

> *'As the church submits to Christ, so also wives should submit to their husbands ____ ____________________.'*
>
> (Ephesians 5:24)

Even though he is head of his home, a man can't possibly make and implement all the decisions necessary for the smooth running of the home and care of the children. His wife is to rule with him. As she carries out her work efficiently and creatively she is a means of God's blessing and favour to her husband.

When a man *knows* that his wife accepts his final authority, he'll be more ready to let her express her creative talents and gifts and he'll be proud of her successes. If he isn't sure of his wife's love and esteem, he may become repressive and suspicious.

A man's reaction to a wife who competes with him for authority in the home is often to limit her freedom and become domineering himself.

Never agree to disagree. In other words, make sure that you sort out differences, not simply sweep them under the carpet. God intended that husband and wife should be a powerful team together. Power is released when they learn to agree and rule *in unity*.

b. At work

A woman can rule at work by seeking to excel in her creative abilities, by mastering the task in hand and by learning to stay calm in difficult and disruptive circumstances.

Once, when Jesus was in a boat with his disciples, there was a violent storm (Mark 4:35-41). Some of these men had spent their working lives fishing on the same lake. They had weathered many storms, but they hadn't learnt the secret of *ruling* in their circumstances. Jesus said to them:

> *'Why are you so afraid? Do you still have no ________?'*
>
> (Mark 4:40)

Learn to rule at work and you'll be a woman who is full of faith instead of fear.

c. In the church

> *'Of the increase of his government and peace there will be no end.'*
>
> (Isaiah 9:7)

In Jesus' kingdom there is government. One dictionary definition for the word 'govern' is 'to exercise continuous sovereign authority over'. As the government or rule of Jesus increases in a person's life, so also does peace.

In the same way, as the church of Jesus Christ moves increasingly in obedience to his Word and authority, so peace will come there (Romans 14:17-18).

Men and women are called to be involved together in the increase of that kingdom. Are you using your God-given intelligence, gifts, abilities, wisdom and talent to serve God's people? By doing so you're ruling alongside the men and so bringing glory to Jesus.

Learn to be an encouragement, strength and support to those whom God has appointed to lead. Be faithful in sharing the insights God gives you in prayer and through the Word.

You have a unique contribution to make to the church. If you don't use it to serve the Lord and his people, you won't be exercising the rule God expects you to bring.

As you initiate new ideas and avenues of service, remember that you haven't been called to 'do your own thing' but to serve Jesus and his purposes. In all you do be ready and willing to submit to the final authority of those whom God has appointed to lead.

It's only as women reflect fully the image and nature of God as he intended it that the church will be made ready as a bride for her heavenly bridegroom, Jesus (Matthew 25:1-13).

LESSON 7

God's Design for Woman: A Mother and Co-Ruler

True or False

1. T F The desire to 'mother' is a natural part of being a woman.
2. T F Single women can never truly be fulfilled.
3. T F Developing new skills and increasing her profitability is part of a woman's commission from God.
4. T F Paid employment provides an excellent opportunity to demonstrate to those who don't know God what he is like.
5. T F When a family is in financial difficulty a wife should always take a job to help out.
6. T F Only men are called to rule.
7. T F Praying for the sick and taking authority over spiritual forces is something that men *and* women can be involved in.
8. T F If a woman isn't prepared to put herself under her husband's authority, she shouldn't get married.
9. T F Being truly submissive means saying nothing and meekly doing all that is required.

10. T F By using her God-given gifts and abilities in the church, a woman can rule alongside the men.

Group Discussion

1. In what specific situations can a woman rule over spiritual powers in her daily life? Give personal testimonies or examples.

2. Let each person share one significant thing that God has spoken to her about through this study.

Personal Assignment

1. In what ways are *you* responding to God's desire for you to be a reflection of his nature in 'mothering', 'subduing' and 'ruling'? Thank God for what he has already done in your life in making you more like him.

2. Write down three specific goals in these areas that you are working towards. Pray about how you are going to achieve them.

True or False

1.T 2.F 3.T 4.T 5.F 6.F 7.T 8.T 9.F 10.T